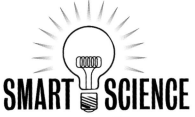

SMART SCIENCE

# Sound and Light

Robert Snedden

**Heinemann Library**
**Des Plaines, Illinois**

Text designed by Visual Image
Cover designed by M2
Illustrations by Paul Bale, Peter Bull and Jane Watkins
Printed in Hong Kong

03 02 01 00 99
10 9 8 7 6 5 4 3 2 1

**Library of Congress Cataloging-in-Publication Data**

Snedden, Robert.
      Sound and light/ Robert Snedden.
      p. cm. -- (Smart science)
    Includes bibliographical references and index.
    Summary: discusses various aspects of light and sound, including noise, color, pitch, loudness, bouncing sound, music, vision, reflection, lenses, and diffraction.
    ISBN 1-57572-870-2 (lib. bdg.)
    1. Light—Juvenile literature. 2. Sound—Juvenile literature.
3. Light—Study and teaching (Elementary)—Activity programs-
–Juvenile literature. 4. Sound—Study and teaching (Elementary)-
–Activity programs—Juvenile literature. [1. Light. 2. Sound.]
    I. Title. II. Series.
    QC360.S64 1999
    535—dc21                          98-49852
                                                  CIP
                                                   AC

**Acknowledgments**
The publisher would like to thank the following for permission to reproduce photographs:
FLPA/Martin Withers, p. 28; J. Allan Cash, pp. 17, 23, 25; Redferns/Simon King, p. 5; David Redferns, p. 9; Mick Hutson, p. 12; Robert Harding Picture Library/Minden Pictures/Flip Nicklin, p. 7; Adam Woolfitt, p. 15; Sally Greenhill, p. 22; Science Photo Library/Milton Heiberg, p. 4; Malcolm Fielding/BOC Group, p. 11; Charles D. Winters, p. 16; Gordon Garradd, p. 20; David Parker, p. 27; Trevor Hill, p. 26.

Cover photograph reproduced with permission of Science Photo Library (Charles D. Winters)

Every effort has been made to contact copyright holders of any material reproduced in this book. Any omissions will be rectified in subsequent printings if notice is given to the Publisher.

**Note to the Reader**
Some words in this book are shown in bold, **like this.** You can find out what they mean by looking in the glossary.

# Contents

# A WORLD OF NOISE AND COLOR

Most people rely on their senses of sight and hearing to understand what is going on in the world around them. The world is a very different place for a person who cannot see or who cannot hear.

## Eyes and Ears

Sound and light may seem to be very different, but they are both forms of **energy**. We learn most of what we know about the world by using two pairs of sensitive energy detectors—our eyes and our ears. Our eyes detect light energy, and our ears detect the energy of sound. They send signals to our brains that let us build up a detailed world of color and noise. Our ears can hear sounds as quiet as a whisper, and our eyes can see the faint light from distant stars.

Sound can carry enough energy to hurt your ears and shake windows, as you know if you've ever heard a low-flying aircraft. The energy in bright sunlight will damage your eyes if you look at it directly, or burn your skin if you are exposed to it for too long.

A firework display brilliantly combines noise and light in a spectacular display.

## Waves

Both sound and light energy travel in **waves**. If you drop a stone into a pool of water, you will see ripples or waves spreading out across the water from the point where the stone went in. The energy that the stone had when it was moving has been transferred to the water. In the same way, when you speak or sing, you send waves of sound energy out through the air. When you turn on a light, waves of light energy flood out in all directions. Knowing that sound and light are waves helps us understand how they act.

Lighting can add to our enjoyment of the sounds of music and theater.

### It's a Fact—At Lightning Speed

Light travels through the air almost a million times faster than sound. That is why you see a lightning flash before you hear the thunder.

### Try This—Seeing Sounds

**You need:** a large can and some grains of rice

**What to do:** Turn the can upside-down on a flat surface. Scatter some grains of rice over the base of the can. Now put your hands close to the can and clap loudly. Do you see the rice grains jump? The sound energy produced by your clap has made them move.

# WHAT IS SOUND?

Take an elastic band and stretch it out. Pluck it with your thumb as you hold it. You can see the band moving rapidly back and forth, and you hear a hum. Now put your finger lightly against your throat and hum a note. Can you feel your Adam's apple moving?

## Vibrations

All sounds are caused by **vibrations**. If you pluck a guitar string, for example, the string vibrates. It moves backward and forward rapidly, and as it does so, it bumps into and pushes the air alongside it, sending **waves** of **energy** through the air.

## Sound Waves

Sound needs something to travel through. The sounds we hear travel through the air to reach our ears. Air is made up of billions and billions of very tiny **molecules** of gas. When you clap your hands, you push some of the air molecules together; these molecules of air then push the molecules of air that are next to them, and so on. A wave of **compressed** molecules passes through the air. If someone else is standing close enough, the wave of compressed air will press on the inside of their ears, and they will hear the sound of your hand clap.

When an object vibrates, it causes air molecules to bunch and move outward as sound waves.

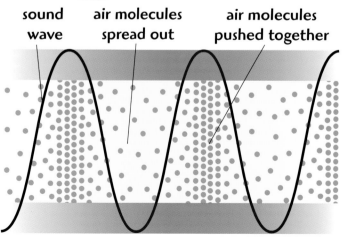

sound wave | air molecules spread out | air molecules pushed together

6

Sounds can also travel through solids and liquids, compressing the molecules together just as they do in air. If you press your ear against a wall in your home, you will be able to hear sounds from the next room. You can also hear sounds if you swim underwater, although they sound a bit odd because our ears are not adapted for hearing in water.

Sound travels much farther underwater. Some whales can send sounds over hundreds of miles through the ocean.

## It's a Fact—Sound Speeds

Sound travels faster through solids than it does through the air. It will travel about twenty times faster through steel than it does through the air.

## Try This—Make a Squeaker

**You need:** a drinking straw and scissors

**What to do:** Use the scissors to cut a small V-shape from the end of the straw. Now pinch the cut ends of the straw together to flatten them. Put the cut end of the straw into your mouth and blow. As you blow, the cut ends vibrate, producing a silly, squeaking noise! You could try making your squeaker louder by making a cone from cardboard to fit over the end of the squeaker.

# HOW WE HEAR

The outer parts of your ears act like satellite dishes, collecting sound **waves** and channeling them inside your ears. The sound waves then reach the **eardrums** and make them vibrate. An eardrum is a membrane rather like the skin of a drum that is stretched across the entrance to the middle ear.

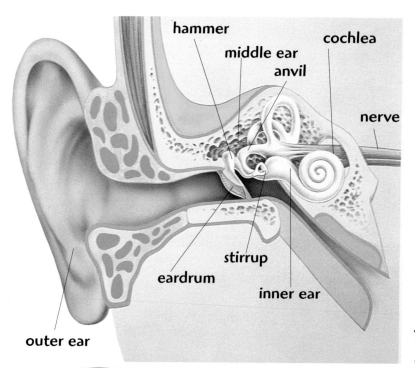

hammer

cochlea

middle ear

anvil

nerve

stirrup

eardrum

inner ear

outer ear

## Inside the Ear

In the middle ear, there are three bones—the hammer, anvil, and stirrup. These are the smallest bones in your body. They transfer the **vibrations** from the eardum to the **cochlea**, one of the most remarkable parts of your body. Nerve endings lining the inside of the cochlea are triggered by the vibrations and fire off signals to your brain. Your brain can then figure out what sort of sound you have heard and where it has come from.

As you can see, there is more to your ear than a flap of skin on the outside of your head!

## Deafness

There are people who were born unable to hear because a part of their ears did not develop properly, and those who have become deaf because their ears have been damaged. If the damage is to the middle ear, but the cochlea still works, some

# It's a Fact—Good Vibrations

World-class **percussionist** Evelyn Glennie has been deaf since the age of twelve. She cannot hear the music she makes but senses the sound vibrations through her hands and feet.

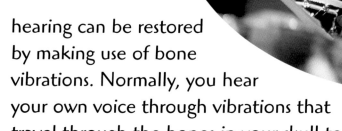

hearing can be restored by making use of bone vibrations. Normally, you hear your own voice through vibrations that travel through the bones in your skull to your inner ear. A deaf person can be fitted with a hearing aid that carries sound directly to the bones in the skull so he or she can hear sounds in the same way you can hear your voice.

## Try This—Make a Telephone

**You need:** two plastic cups, a long piece of string, a sharp pencil, and a friend

**What to do:** Make a hole in the bottom of each cup using the pencil. Tie a knot in one end of the string and feed the other end through the holes in the cups. Tie

a knot in the other end of the string to make sure that the cup will not slip off the end. Give one cup to a friend. Then stretch the string tightly between you. Get your friend to put the cup to his or her ear while you talk into your cup. The sound vibrations travel along the string to the plastic cup and into your friend's ear, where they can be heard.

# PITCH AND LOUDNESS

Just like the **waves** on the sea, sound and light waves also have high points, called crests, and low points, called troughs.

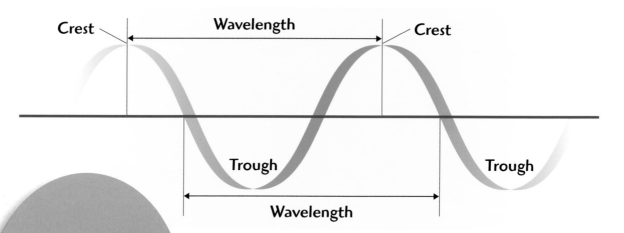

**Waves of energy rise and fall, forming regular peaks and troughs.**

## Wavelength and Frequency

**Wavelength** is the distance from one wave crest to another. The **frequency** of a wave is the number of crests that pass by a given point in a second. From one wave crest to another is a cycle, and frequency is measured in cycles per second, or **hertz**. All sound waves travel through the air at the same speed. A sound with a long wavelength will have a low frequency, because it takes longer for a single wave to pass by. A short wavelength means a high frequency because more waves can pass by in a given time.

## High and Low

We usually talk about the **pitch** of a sound rather than its frequency. Sounds can be either high or low. A high-pitched sound, such as a whistle, has a high frequency (and short waves). A low-pitched sound,

Loud noises from heavy machinery can be harmful to the people operating it. Ear protectors prevent damage to their ears.

like the rumble of traffic on a distant road, has a low frequency (and long waves). As people get older, they tend to lose the ability to hear higher-pitched sounds.

## Loudness

How loud a sound is depends on how much **energy** the sound waves carry. The more energy the sound waves have, the more they will make your **eardrums** vibrate and the louder it will sound. Loudness can make the pitch of a sound seem different. A loud, low-pitched sound will seem even lower, while a loud, high-pitched sound seems even higher.

## It's a Fact—High Frequency

The human ear can detect sounds of around 20,000 cycles per second. Some bats can hear sounds with frequencies up to 120,000 cycles per second.

## Try This—Musical Bottles

**You need:** several empty bottles of the same size, a jug of water

**What to do:** Place the bottles in a row. Leave the first bottle empty. Pour a little water into the next bottle, a little more in the one after that, and so on, until the last bottle is nearly full. Tap the bottles or blow across their necks. Which bottle gives the highest pitched sound and which the lowest? The shorter the column of air, the smaller the waves it makes, and the higher pitched the sounds will be.

# BOUNCING SOUNDS

The study of sound and how it travels is called **acoustics**. Sound **waves** travel in straight lines from the source of the sound. When they strike objects, they may be either reflected or absorbed.

## Echoes

If you stand at a distance from a hard, flat surface, such as a cliff or the side of a building, and shout toward it, you will hear the sound of your shout bouncing back to you as an **echo**. So why isn't the world a confusion of echoing sounds? The first reason is that not all surfaces reflect sounds. Soft surfaces absorb sounds, so no echo bounces back. The second reason is that if two sounds happen less than a tenth of a second apart, our ears hear them as a single sound. An echo coming less than a tenth of a second after the sound that made it adds to the original sound, making it appear to last longer. This is called **reverberation**.

**Specially designed sound reflectors in the ceiling help everyone to hear the concert.**

# Sound Design

Architects who design concert halls and theaters have to consider the acoustics of the building. They want everyone in the hall to be able to hear the performers clearly without any distracting echoes. This does not mean that they want to get rid of echoes altogether. Sounds heard in a room with no reverberation sound dull and lifeless. Panels are carefully positioned to reflect sound toward the audience. This makes the sound seem to reverberate as the reflected sounds add to the original ones. Too much reverberation can make sounds appear confused, so other sound-absorbing panels are positioned to control the reverberation.

## It's a Fact—Ultrasound

Doctors can use the echoes from a very high frequency sound, called ultrasound, to form a picture of the inside of the human body.

## Try This—Ticking Tubes

**You need:** two long cardboard tubes, a table, a large piece of stiff cardboard, modeling clay, and a watch that ticks

**What to do:** Stand the cardboard upright on the table, holding it in place with the modeling clay. Position the tubes so they are pointing toward the cardboard and at an angle to each other, with a gap about 2 in. (5 cm) between the ends of the tubes and the cardboard. Place a watch at the end of a tube farthest from the cardboard and listen at the end of the other tube. You should hear the ticking of the watch clearly through your tube. The sound travels down one tube and is reflected from the cardboard and into the second tube.

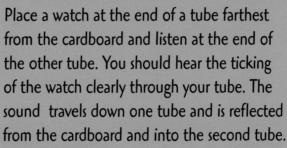

# MUSIC

What is the difference between music and noise? Is there some quality that music has that allows us to say that a sound is musical, even if we do not happen to like it?

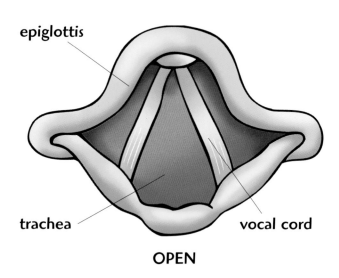

epiglottis

trachea

vocal cord

OPEN

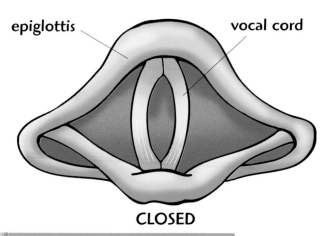

epiglottis

vocal cord

CLOSED

## Tone

Musical sounds are called **tones**. Musical tones, like other sounds, are made by **vibrations**. The difference between a musical tone and a noise is that the vibrations in a tone are regular. When you cough, you send an uncontrolled surge of air through the **vocal cords** in your throat, causing a great mixture of vibrations. When you sing, you force air between the vocal cords in a controlled way, making them vibrate in a more regular way, and producing a much nicer sound.

Opening the vocal cords produces a low-pitched sound, and pulling them closed makes a high-pitched sound.

## Making Music

Musical instruments make sounds in one of three ways. In a guitar, violin, or piano, you make a string vibrate by plucking it, by striking it, or by drawing a bow across it. The vibration of the string causes the sound box of the instrument to vibrate.

Percussion instruments, such as drums, depend on making a solid surface vibrate. A xylophone, for example, is made up of different-sized bars of wood. When you strike one of these wooden bars with a soft hammer, the bar vibrates.

Wind instruments make sounds when the air inside them vibrates. Trumpets, trombones, flutes, and recorders are all wind instruments.

The different instruments of an orchestra combine to give a rich blend of sounds.

## It's a Fact—Making Music

People have been making music for a long time. Musical instruments have been found that are over 30,000 years old.

## Try This—A Rubber Band!

**You need:** rubber bands of various thicknesses, twelve brads, scissors, and an old shoe box

**What to do:** Push the brads into the ends of the shoe box lid, six at each end. Cut a circular hole in the lid and put it back on the box. Stretch the rubber bands over the top of the hole in the lid and secure them at each end with the brads. Fold the edges of the cut-out circle up to make a bridge to raise your "strings" above the box. Place the bridge under the bands at one end of the box. Pluck the bands with your fingers. To make higher notes, try tightening the bands by turning the brads.

# WHAT IS LIGHT?

If you stand outside on a sunny day, you can feel the sun's **energy** warming your skin. During the day, all of the light we have outside comes from the sun.

## Glowing Hot

When something gets hot, it begins to give off energy in the form of heat. The hotter it gets, the more energy it gives off. If an object is heated to a temperature of about 900°F (500°C), some of the energy it gives off takes the form of light. It begins to glow a dull cherry red. If the temperature rises still more, the object will glow steadily brighter. The surface of the sun is at a temperature of about 10,000°F (5,500°C), and it glows white hot, sending **waves** of light energy out into space in all directions.

## Shadow Show

Light waves always travel along straight paths. You can see straight rays of light when the sun shines through gaps in broken clouds. Shadows are formed when light rays are blocked by a solid object, such as a tree or a person. The size of the shadow depends on how close the object blocking the light is to the source of the light. When the object is far away from the light source, the shadow is small because little light is blocked out. An object near the light source will block a lot of light and so make a big shadow.

The **filament** inside a light bulb glows brightly as it heats up.

# It's a Fact— The Speed of Light

Light is the fastest thing in the **universe**— nothing can travel faster. Light from the sun crosses 93 million miles (150 million kilometers) of nearly empty space to reach us in just 8 minutes. Light travels at nearly 186,000 miles (300,000 kilometers) per second.

## Try This—Make a Shadow Portrait

**You need:** large sheets of paper, a smooth wall in bright sunshine, tape, a pencil, and a friend

**What to do:** Tape the paper to the wall. Then have a friend stand sideways near the wall so that the shadow of his or her head falls onto the paper. Sketch around the outside of the shadow. Cut out the shadow portrait. Does it look like the person? Try doing portraits with the person in different positions to see how the shadow changes.

# THE WAY WE SEE

We can see the world around us because light is reflected from the objects we are looking at.

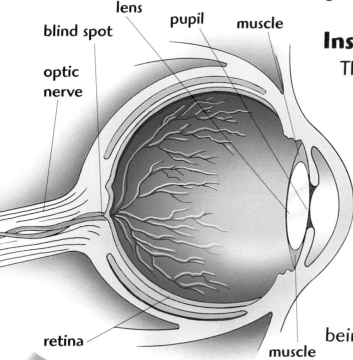

blind spot

lens

pupil

muscle

optic nerve

retina

muscle

## Inside the Eye

The dark area in the center of your eye is your **pupil**. It can become bigger or smaller to control the amount of light that gets into your eye. In dim light, the pupil opens up to let as much light as possible into your eye. In bright sunlight, the pupil is small to limit the amount of light. This prevents you from being dazzled in bright sunlight.

The human eye is a tough, fluid-filled ball sitting inside a bony socket in the skull.

Light enters the eye through a clear **lens** that sits just behind the pupil. The lens in your eye is held in place by muscles that can adjust the shape of the lens, allowing you to focus on objects at different distances. These muscles work so well that you can glance up from your book to look at a tree in the distance, for example, and see it sharply right away.

The lens directs the light onto the **retina**. The retina is a sensitive layer at the back of the eye that reacts to light. As light strikes different parts of the retina, signals are sent to the brain. The brain puts these signals together to form a picture.

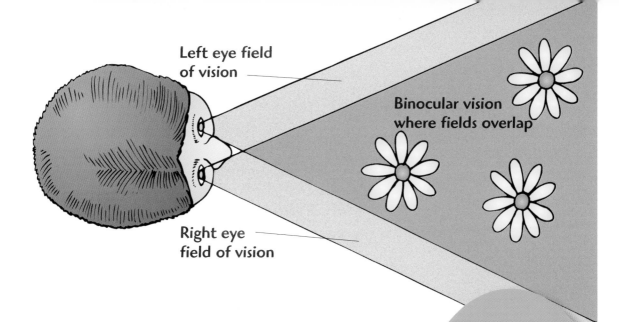

Left eye field of vision

Binocular vision where fields overlap

Right eye field of vision

## Binocular Vision

Each eye sends a slightly different image to the brain. You can see this for yourself. Close one eye and line up a finger with a distant object. Now, without moving the finger, open the other eye and close the first one. The finger is no longer lined up. This is because each eye sees an object from a slightly different angle and at a slightly different place in its **field of vision**. The brain forms one three-dimensional image from the two images it receives from the eyes. This is called **binocular vision**. It allows us to judge how far away an object is.

Each eye gives a slightly different view of the world. The fields of vision overlap, helping us judge distance and depth.

### It's a Fact—Eye Exercises

The focusing muscles around the lenses of your eyes adjust around 100,000 times every day.

### Try This—Near or Far?

**You need:** a pen with a top

**What to do:** Hold the pen at arm's length and take the top off. Now put it back on. Easy, wasn't it? Now try doing it with one eye closed. It isn't so easy now, is it? Your brain can only judge distance by having slightly different images from each eye to compare.

# Color

The white light from the sun is actually a combination of different colors called the **spectrum**. A rainbow is a spectrum of light in the sky. Light from the sun bounces back to your eyes after having been reflected from raindrops in the air. Each color in the spectrum is reflected back at a slightly different angle, and they spread out to form the rainbow in which all the colors of the spectrum are visible.

## Changing Color

Objects can appear to change color if you look at them through a colored **filter**, such as a sheet of plastic or cellophane. The filter will only let light that is the same color as itself pass through. A green filter only lets green light through, for instance, making everything look green or black. If you look at a red object through a green filter, it appears black because the filter blocks the red light reflecting from the object. You might try putting some colored cellophane over a flashlight to make different colored lights and see how things look when you shine your light on them.

Raindrops split sunlight up into a spectrum so we see a rainbow.

## Primary Colors

Red, green, and blue are often called the primary colors of light. Other colors can be made by mixing the primary colors. Red and green light mixed together will make yellow; red and blue make magenta; blue and green make cyan. When all three primary colors are mixed in equal amounts, they produce white light. The primary colors of paints and dyes are yellow, magenta, and cyan—the three colors made by mixing the primary light colors! Mixing all three primary paint colors will make black, rather than white.

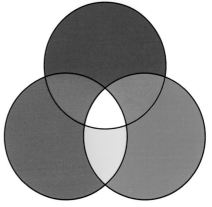

the effect of mixing light

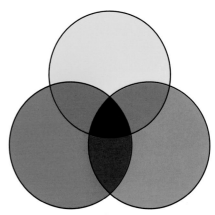

the effect of mixing paint

Mixing the primary light colors produces the primary colors of paints and dyes.

## It's a Fact—Flying Colors

Many flying insects see not only the colors we can see. They also see **ultraviolet light**, sometimes called "bee purple," which is often reflected by flower petals.

## Try This—See a Spectrum

**You need:**  water in a straight-sided glass, a piece of cardboard with a vertical slit in it about a half-inch (a centimeter) wide, scotch tape, a sheet of white paper, and a sunny window

**What to do:**  Tape the cardboard with the vertical slit to the side of the glass. Put the glass near a window so the light shines through the slit. As the beam of light passes through the water, it splits into a rainbow of colors. Put the white paper under the glass to make the colors stand out more.

# ON REFLECTION

You probably see your **reflection** several times every day. You may see it in the bathroom mirror as you brush your teeth, or catch sight of it in a window as you walk by. Why do some objects produce better reflections than others? Why do some objects produce no reflections at all?

## Surface Appearances

All objects reflect light. If they did not, we would not be able to see them. Most things do not have flat surfaces. They are rough and uneven, and light bounces off them in all directions. A smooth surface forms a reflection because it reflects the light that strikes it evenly. The shinier the surface, the clearer the image will be.

## Mirrors

You can see yourself in a mirror because light bounces from you to the mirror and then from the mirror into your eyes. Any smooth surface that will reflect light can be a mirror. Most mirrors we use are made of very smooth, polished glass. A thin film of silver or aluminium is laid on the back of the glass to give a particularly smooth surface. It is this backing that acts as the reflecting surface.

The image you see in a mirror appears to be reversed, left to right.

Curved mirrors are used to direct light rays in particular directions. Look inside the front of a flashlight, and you will see that there is a shiny curved surface around the flashlight bulb. This acts to focus the light into a single powerful beam. A car headlight also has a curved back of polished metal that acts like a mirror, directing the light from the bulb in a beam that will shine straight out in front of the car, lighting up the road ahead.

**A curved, reflective surface around a car headlight is used to focus light in a tight beam.**

## It's a Fact—A Mirror to the Stars

The Keck telescope in Hawaii has a curved mirror 33 feet (10 meters) across to gather the faint light from distant stars.

## Try This—Make a Periscope

**You need:** two small mirrors, a cardboard tube, modeling clay, scotch tape, and scissors

**What to do:** Cut a hole in each end of the tube. Put a mirror at an angle in each hole. Adjust the angles of the mirrors until you can see each mirror reflected in the other one. Hold the mirrors in position with clay and scotch tape. If you hold the periscope up and look in the bottom hole, you will see the view from the hole in the top. It is as if you were able to hold your eyes above your head.

# LOOKING AT LENSES

Light may be the fastest thing in the **universe**, but it does not always travel at the same speed. When light **waves** pass from one **transparent** material to another, from air to glass for example, they change speed.

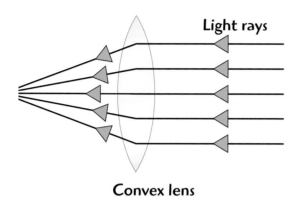

Light rays

Convex lens

## Refraction

When a beam of light passes from air into a liquid, such as water, or a clear solid, such as glass, it is slowed down. When it passes back into the air again, it speeds up. The effect of this is that the light beam is bent. This is called **refraction**.

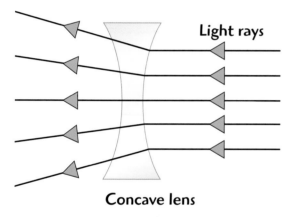

Light rays

Concave lens

## Bringing It into Focus

**Lenses** are specially shaped pieces of glass or plastic that are used to bend the light passing through them in useful ways. A **convex** lens is thickest in the middle and curves in towards the edges. It is used to bend light rays inwards, bringing them to a point, called a focus. A magnifying glass is a type of convex lens. It makes objects seen through it look bigger.

A convex lens will bend light rays inwards, whereas a concave lens will spread the rays out.

Concave lenses are thicker at the edges and curve in towards the middle. A concave lens bends light outwards, making objects seen through it look smaller.

## Seeing More Clearly

The lenses in the eyes of many people do not focus light properly. The lenses cannot focus a sharp image on the **retina**. Nearsighted people have the problem that light is focused just in front of the retina rather than on it. Glasses with concave lenses can help by spreading the beams of light out slightly before they enter the eye. The eye's lens then focuses the beams correctly on the retina. Farsighted people focus light beyond the retina. Convex lenses are used to help them bring the focus forward onto the retina.

Giant lenses like this one focus the beam of a lighthouse, sending the beam a long distance across the sea.

## Try This—Make a Microscope

**You need:** two magnifying glasses, or a magnifying glass and an old camera lens

**What to do:** Microscopes use two or more lenses to give greater magnification than you could get with just one lens. Hold one magnifying glass close to your eye and hold the other just above the object you want to look at—just about 20 to 23 in. (50 to 60 cm) from your eye. Move the lenses up and down slightly until you see a sharp image of the object.

25

# PATTERNS OF LIGHT

Have you ever noticed the swirling patterns of color on the surface of a soap bubble? These are caused by an effect called **interference**.

## Patterns of Light

Light **waves** are not all the same size. Different colors have different-sized waves and different frequencies. When light passes through a bubble, the rays are reflected in different directions from the outside, and from the inside, of the bubble. A ray of light coming back toward your eye from the inside of the bubble has slightly farther to travel than one being reflected from the outside. When the two rays meet, they interfere with each other. Some colors cancel each other out, and others join together. The result is that shifting bands of color appear on the bubble's surface.

The shifting colors that can be seen on the surface of a bubble are interference patterns.

# Diffraction

Rays of light will also bend slightly as they pass around the edge of an object that is in their path. You can see this when light travels through a narrow slit. As it does so, it spreads out slightly. This is called **diffraction**. Light beams bent in this way will interfere with each other to form colored patterns. If you nearly close your eyes and look at a light through your eyelashes, you may be able to see the colored patterns that form as the light bends around your eyelashes.

When white light shines through a triangular glass prism, it splits into the colors of the spectrum.

## It's a Fact—Light Waves

In 1803, Thomas Young (1773–1829) proved that light was like a wave by showing how it made interference patterns. He was a gifted child who could read by the age of two. He spoke eight languages by the age of fourteen.

## Try This—Bubble People

**You need:** a length of flexible wire, a strong soap solution made from dish soap liquid, sugar, and a bowl

**What to do:** Pour the soap solution into the bowl. (Mixing in a couple of spoonfuls of the sugar will give a thicker solution.) Bend the wire to make the shape of a person. Dip the wire into the soap solution and draw it out carefully. A film of soap forms inside the figure. You will see colored bands of light moving in your figure as the soap film reflects and interferes with the light.

# SEEING IS BELIEVING?

We can see the world around us because light forms an image that we see with our eyes and our brain. But can we always believe what we see?

## Look Again

As you grow up and learn about the world, your brain builds up a store of information. You learn that far-away objects look smaller than objects that are near. Your brain can be tricked if you look at something that is not quite what it seems.

The lake that these antelope appear to be grazing by is, in fact, a mirage.

On very hot days, you may sometimes see what appears to be a pool of water on the road ahead of you. This is a **mirage**. A layer of hot air forms just above the ground, and the light from the sky reflects off it. Since you do not expect to see blue sky on the ground, your brain interprets what it sees as water. A second kind of mirage can occur in very cold regions where the air close to the ground is colder than the air higher up. The warmer air can act like a mirror in the sky, reflecting back images of distant objects. Ships and icebergs can seem to be floating in the air!

The first movie audiences were fascinated by the magic of the moving image.

## Making Movies

Every time you go to the movies, you are playing a trick on your eyes. A strip of cinema film is a series of still images, each one slightly different from the one before it. When the film is run through the projector, we see the images very quickly, one after the other, at a rate of 24 images per second. The brain cannot distinguish images that come that fast, and it runs them together so that we think the pictures are really moving.

**Try This—Make a Cartoon Book**

**You need:** a notebook and a pencil

**What to do:** At the top corner of each page of the notebook, make a little drawing of a figure doing something, such as bouncing a ball or walking. On each page, make the position of the figure slightly different. The figure might take one step, then another. When you have filled the book, flip through the pages rapidly with your thumb. Your figure should appear to move.

# GLOSSARY

**acoustics**   study of sound and how it travels within a space, such as a room or concert hall

**binocular vision**   ability to see depth and judge distance based on the images received by both eyes

**cochlea**   part of the inner ear that detects sound vibrations and sends information to the brain

**compressed**   squeezed together

**concave**   describes a lens that curves inwards

**convex**   describes a lens that curves outwards from the center

**diffraction**   the spreading out of **waves** when they pass through a narrow opening

**eardrum**   part of the middle ear that vibrates from sound waves

**echo**   sound that is reflected from something so you hear it again

**energy**   ability to do work

**field of vision**   space within which objects are visible without moving your eyes or head

**filament**   thin wire in a light bulb that glows as electricity passes through it

**filter**   object that lets through some things but not others; a red filter will let through red light but not green, for example

**frequency**   number of waves that pass a particular point in a second

**hertz**   unit of frequency, equal to one cycle per second

**interference**   what happens when light waves of the same **frequency** meet each other and combine together

**lens**   something that can change the direction of beams of light, spreading them out or bringing them to a point

**mirage**   optical illusion caused by light reflecting or bending as it passes through different layers of air

**molecules**   very tiny particles that are the smallest parts of all elements or compounds

**percussion/percussionist** musical instruments played by striking them. A person who plays a percussion instrument is called a percussionist.

**pitch** quality of a sound that makes it high or low

**pupil** circular opening in the eye through which light enters

**reflection** the way light or sound bounces back

**refraction** bending of light as it travels from one transparent material to another

**retina** light-sensitive layer on the inside of the eye that sends signals to the brain

**reverberation** what happens when an **echo** reaches you before the original sound has ended, making the first sound seem longer

**spectrum** spread of colors that white light can be split into (red, orange, yellow, green, blue, indigo, and violet)

**tones** distinctive sounds of musical instruments

**transparent** substance through which light can pass easily

**ultraviolet light** an invisible (to humans) part of the light **spectrum** that comes after violet

**universe** all of space and everything in it—including us

**vibration** fast, regular back and forth movement

**vocal cords** folds inside your throat that vibrate when air passes over them, making the sound of your voice

**wave** regular disturbance carrying energy through a medium, such as sound through air, or light across space

**wavelength** distance between the crest of one wave and the crest of the next one

# MORE BOOKS TO READ

Ardley, Neil. *Sound Waves to Music: Projects with Sound.* Danbury, CT: Franklin Watts. 1990.

Branley, Franklyn M. *Light & Darkness.* New York: HarperCollins Children's Books. 1998.

Dixon, Malcolm & Karen Smith. *Light & Color.* Mankato, MN: Smart Apple Media. 1998.

Glover, David M. *The Super Science Book of Sound.* Chatham, NJ: Raintree Steck-Vaughn. 1994.

Kerrod, Robin. *Light & Sound.* Tarrytown, NY: Marshall Cavendish. 1995.

Lauber, Patricia. *What Do You See?* New York: Crown Books for Young Readers. 1994.

Reddy, Francis & Isaac Abella. *Discover Light & Sound.* Lake Forest, IL: Forest House Publishing. 1996.

Rowe, Julian. *Music.* Des Plaines, Illinois Heinemann Library. 1997.

Wood, Robert W. *Light Fundamentals.* Broomall, PA: Chelsea House. 1997.

Wood, Robert W. *Sound Fundamentals.* Broomall, PA: Chelsea House. 1997.

# INDEX